W9-AAO-247

OFFICE MANAGEMENT

A Productivity And Effectiveness Guide

Marilyn Manning, Ph.D.

Patricia Haddock

CRISP PUBLICATIONS, INC.
Los Altos, California

OFFICE MANAGEMENT
A Productivity And Effectiveness Guide

Marilyn Manning, Ph.D.
Patricia Haddock

CREDITS
Editor: **Michael G. Crisp**
Designer: **Carol Harris**
Typesetting: **Interface Studio**
Cover Design: **Carol Harris**
Artwork: **Ralph Mapson**

The cartoon on the cover has been reprinted by permission of the author Sidney Harris and is from the book, ''WHAT'S SO FUNNY ABOUT BUSINESS?'', ©1986 William Kaufmann, Inc., 95 First Street, Los Altos, CA 94022.

All rights reserved. No part of this book may be reproduced or transmitted in any form or by any means now known or to be invented, electronic or mechanical, including photocopying, recording, or by any information storage or retrieval system without written permission from the author or publisher, except for the brief inclusion of quotations in a review.

Copyright © 1990 by Crisp Publications, Inc.
Printed in the United States of America

Crisp books are distributed in Canada by Reid Publishing, Ltd., P.O. Box 7267, Oakville, Ontario, Canada L6J 6L6.

In Australia by Career Builders, P.O. Box 1051, Springwood, Brisbane, Queensland, Australia 4127.

And in New Zealand by Career Builders, P.O. Box 571, Manurewa, New Zealand.

Library of Congress Catalog Card Number 89-81242
Manning, Marilyn and Haddock, Patricia
Office Management: A Productivity And Effectiveness Guide
ISBN 1-56052-005-1

INTRODUCTION

Being an office manager is not an easy task. It requires a variety of skills and a lot of patience. For example:

• You must be an effective planner, for both short- and long-term. You must take appropriate actions to ensure your plans are met, and be flexible enough to change plans and actions as necessary.

• You must also be a people-person, capable of putting together effective teams when required to get the job done. This involves hiring, training, evaluating, and coaching employees. You must be adept at delegation skills.

• You must develop standards and controls to ensure those involved contribute to office productivity and work toward the goals of your organization.

• You must communicate effectively to get the results you need to achieve. You must know how to manage and resolve conflict, and negotiate solutions that result in win-win situations for everyone.

• And if that's not enough, you have to make sure your customers and co-workers have their needs met and are kept happy.

This book will help you do all of the above. It will teach you new skills or reinforce skills you already have.

Read it through and perform the exercises. Then continue to use it as a reference when situations arise that need special attention.

We wish you luck and good reading.

Marilyn Manning, Ph.D.

Patricia Haddock

DEDICATION

To Seth, Melissa and Scott Manning for their valuable support.

To my mom and my sister, Bev
for their belief in me all these years.

CONTENTS

CONTENTS (Continued)

S E C T I O N *1*

YOUR ROLE AS AN OFFICE MANAGER

THE BUCK STOPS (ALMOST) HERE!

HEATHER

> ''*Office.* Noun. A place where a particular kind of business is transacted or a service is supplied.''
>
> *Webster's New Collegiate Dictionary*

WHAT IS YOUR ROLE?

Every office needs someone who can manage the three W's:
    Workers
                Workflow
                        Workplace

so that customers* receive quality service and the business is a success.

That "someone" is the office manager.

That "someone" is YOU.

> Your job is to manage your workers, the workflow, and the workplace so that external customers receive quality service and your company makes a profit.

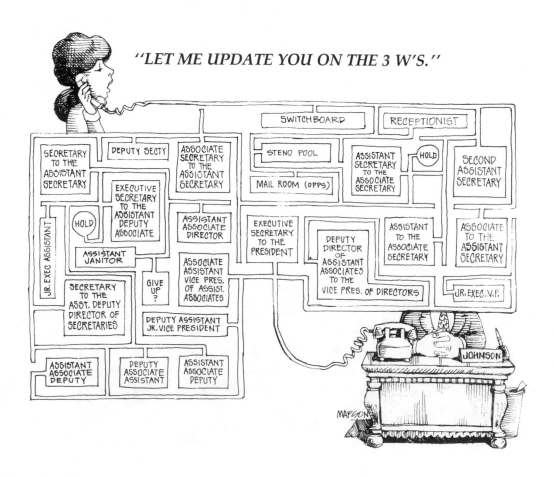

"LET ME UPDATE YOU ON THE 3 W'S."

---

*Throughout the remainder of this book, the term "customer" also includes "clients" for providers of professional services.

WHAT IS AN OFFICE?

An office takes many forms depending on the business it supports.

An accounting office is different from a restaurant supply company office or a medical clinic office. But regardless of the business being transacted, the main function of an office is to provide service to customers, clients, or guests.

In this book customers are considered as both external and internal.

External customers are people and organizations that currently use your company's services or buy its products, and people and organizations that may become customers or clients in the future.

Internal customers are fellow workers. But even if your office exists solely to provide support services to fellow workers, your ultimate goal is still to provide service to your "customers," internal or external!

Keeping customers happy with your organization's services and products is critical to your personal success as an office manager.

ANALYZING YOUR OFFICE

To ensure that everyone in your office is working toward the same goals, each person should be able to complete the following two statements. If you have employees who don't know who your customers are, or how customers are supported, you might want to publish the answers so that everyone knows why your office exists.

1. Our customers are: _____ .

2. Our office supports our customers in these primary ways:

_____

_____

_____

_____

_____

EVALUATING YOUR SUCCESS

As an office manager, you need to accurately evaluate your success in supporting customers. Complete the following statements about how successful your office is in providing customer service:

1. My office is doing better _____ or worse _____ than last year because:

_____

_____

_____

_____

_____

_____

2. My office can better service our customers in the following ways:

_____

_____

_____

_____

_____

_____

Adapted from PROFESSIONAL EXCELLENCE FOR SECRETARIES, by Carolyn Barnes, MA, and Marilyn Manning, Ph.D. For ordering information, see the back of this book.

GUIDELINES FOR OFFICE MANAGEMENT

Do you	Yes	No	Sometimes
Take risks?			
Enjoy your work?			
Establish accountability?			
Avoid blame?			
Plan ahead?			
''Sell'' your ideas?			
Take responsibility?			
Support innovation?			
Encourage creativity?			
Balance direction and autonomy?			
Set goals?			
Build teams?			
Delegate?			
Motivate effectively?			
Support the growth of others?			
Learn from mistakes?			
Juggle multiple tasks?			
Create a pleasant workplace?			
Communicate your vision?			
Strengthen others' sense of worth?			
Behave ethically?			
Expect ethical behavior from others?			
Manage by example?			
Celebrate team wins?			
Recognize the contributions of others?			

If you checked any ''No'' boxes, you have identified areas that seem to need improvement. If you checked ''Sometimes'', read carefully those parts of this book that address these issues. Choose three characteristics to work on and write them below. Then list an action step you will take within the next week to help develop this characteristic.

Characterstic

1. _____

2. _____

3. _____

Action Step

1. _____

2. _____

3. _____

YOUR MAJOR ACTIVITIES AS AN OFFICE MANAGER

Planning: Creating a design for future action.

Organizing: Identifying and allocating all necessary resources.

Decision making: Researching relevant situations and choosing a course of action.

Communicating: Giving and receiving feedback.

Motivating: Using human relation skills to stimulate employee productivity.

Acting: Implementing plans and decisions.

Controlling: Measuring performance against plans.

Evaluating: Analyzing results versus effort, time, and cost.

Leading: Demonstrating by example that your office team is productive, professional, and positive.

BECOMING AN EFFECTIVE OFFICE PLANNER

As an office manager, one of your primary goals is to satisfactorily fulfill your responsibilities. This includes how to meet the needs of both customers and employees. This means you must assess where things stand, formulate some goals, and design short- and long-range plans to achieve your objectives.

Planning never stops. It is the bridge that connects where you are to where you want to be.

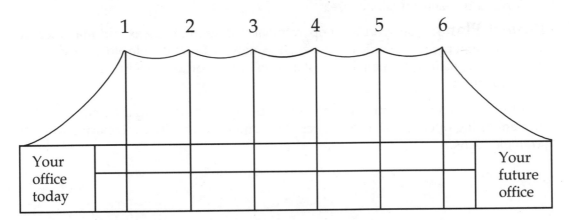

> Plans should be concrete, specific, action-oriented, proactive, understandable, and ethical.

Steps To Be Taken In Order To Build Your Bridge To Your "Future" Office

1 = Collecting information

2 = Forecasting possible future events based on (1)

3 = Creating an image of the future based on (2)

4 = Establishing achievable goals based on (3)

5 = Developing plans to reach the goals chosen in (4)

6 = Monitoring the progress and obtaining feedback on the plans developed in (5)

A SYSTEM OF PLANS

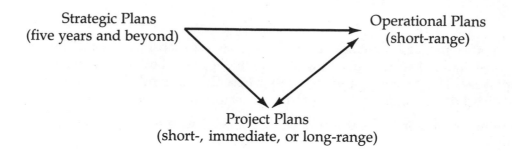

Strategic Plans
(five years and beyond)

Operational Plans
(short-range)

Project Plans
(short-, immediate, or long-range)

Strategic Plans: define broad goals and their implementation over the long-term. They normally come from the organization's top management.

Operational Plans: support strategic plans and outline actions to be performed by each functional area.

Project Plans: support both operational and strategic plans and may include action statements for specific events such as new product development, office productivity, facilities expansion, installation of new office systems, or reorganization.

As office manager, you probably will be responsible for developing and implementing operational and project plans and occasionally contributing to strategic plans.

GOAL SETTING

GOAL SETTING

1. Write a statement of your company's philosophy or mission statement. Example:"Provide our customers with the highest quality processed photographic prints, at competitive prices, within one hour of drop-off."

    Write yours: _____

    _____

    _____

2. Give one example of a short-term goal, i.e., "Design a new promotional direct market self-mailer or product Y before the end the week and stay within budget."

    Write a short-term goal and your plan to achieve this goal:

    _____

    _____

3. Give one example of a long-term goal, i.e., "Have all front-line employees attend a three-hour customer service training course before June 1."

    Write a long-term goal and your plan to achieve this goal:

    _____

    _____

4. Write a personal goal that relates to your job. Example: "Insure the phone is always politely answered before the third ring."

    Write your personal goal: _____

    _____

    _____

(continued next page)

5. Give an example of
    (a) a weekly office goal, i.e., "Send out an average of 25 informational product packages to potential customers each day."

My goal is: _____

_____

_____

My plan(s) to achieve this goal is: _____

_____

_____

    (b) a monthly office goal, i.e., "Update all computer database files by the end of the month."

My goal is: _____

_____

_____

My plan(s) to achieve this goal is: _____

_____

_____

    (c) a quarterly office goal, i.e., "Generate quarterly sales reports and mail to the field within three working days following the end of the quarter."

My goal is: _____

_____

_____

My plan(s) to achieve this goal is: _____

_____

_____

    (d) a yearly office goal, i.e., "Construct and adhere to yearly budget which reflects a 15% productivity improvement per employee."

My goal is: _____

_____

_____

My plan(s) to achieve this goal is: _____

_____

_____

THE ART OF BUYING FOR THE OFFICE

One important job you may have is the responsibility to order equipment, furniture, and supplies for your office. This task gives you an opportunity to demonstrate your value to the organization by controlling what you buy and how much you pay for it. A good manager can help increase organizational profits through intelligent comparision shopping and buying.

Small companies usually depend on someone untrained to buy supplies. Since the cost of the same supplies/equipment can vary up to 60% among vendors, a simple process of obtaining quotes can result in immediate cost savings.

To avoid paying a premium, try these simple steps:

1. Decide what you need, how much you need, and how often you need it.

2. Identify what quote information you need.

3. Obtain quotes from vendors. Ask about volume discounts or special sales.

4. Evaluate the price, quality and service for the merchandise.

5. Purchase from vendors who give you the best price and service for the product.

6. Assign responsibility for purchasing to an employee qualified for the task.

7. Monitor purchasing decisions regularly.

OFFICE EXPENSE ACCOUNTS

Every office needs guidelines for office expense accounts. In larger companies, travel expenses often represent a major corporate expense. Expenses add to administrative overhead and directly affect the bottom line—positively or negatively—depending on how well they are monitored and controlled.

Office managers should be aware of internal policies and procedures regarding expense accounts to ensure only appropriate expenses, directly related to business needs, are reimbursed. Thoughtful controls can add significantly to your organization's financial health.

Here are some recommendations to control expenses. Check those you currently use. As office manager, I:

☐ 1. Tie all expenses to business needs.

☐ 2. Set dollar limits for certain items, such as business lunches, gifts for customers, and non-routine purchases.

☐ 3. Limit corporate credit cards. People tend to spend less if they are using their own money, even if the expenses will be reimbursed via the office expense account.

☐ 4. Encourage comparison shopping, especially in special air fares, major hotel promotions, and car rentals.

☐ 5. Require approval for items that exceed a set dollar amount.

☐ 6. I also:

_____

_____

_____

_____

_____

DRESS CODES

Clothes say a great deal about an individual. People often dress in ways that reflect their feelings of self-worth. As an office manager, your personal dress code communicates much about how you expect your office to look.

The dress code should reflect the job being performed. If you manage a backroom function and your employees do not have direct customer contact, a more casual dress code may be appropriate. If your employees work directly with customers, you will always want to reflect the best possible image. Customer contact employees should dress to make the customer feel comfortable and reflect their competence and expertise.

Remember, it is impossible to create a second "first impression."

DRESS CODE QUESTIONNAIRE

Answer these questions to establish an appropriate dress code for your office.

1. What kind of image do you want to create, (i.e., how do you want others to view your office environment?). _____

_____

_____

2. What attire would make your customers/clients feel comfortable?

_____

_____

_____

3. Do you need separate dress codes for parts of your office?

_____

_____

_____

4. Are uniforms required for some/all of your employees?

_____

_____

_____

5. Does your dress code discriminate because of gender?

_____

_____

_____

6. If possible, does the dress code allow for personal preference?

_____

_____

_____

Add your own: _____

_____

_____

_____

SECTION 2

PERSONNEL-RELATED ACTIVITIES

"Teamwork. noun. Work done by several associates with each doing a part but all subordinating personal prominence to the efficiency of the whole."

Webster's New Collegiate Dictionary

SEVEN RULES FOR TEAMS

An effective office manager doesn't work alone. Effective managers are team leaders, pulling office workers together to meet common goals. There are seven basic rules of team leaders.*

RULE 1: Make sure goals are clearly communicated and understood.

RULE 2: Provide opportunities to meet and exchange ideas with team members.

RULE 3: Treat employees with equal respect and give each an opportunity to make a personal contribution to the outcome.

RULE 4: Set a good example by supporting company policies and procedures.

RULE 5: Act consistently and positively.

RULE 6: Stay calm under pressure.

RULE 7: Keep all promises made to team members.

Identify three ways you can begin to apply these rules immediately and write them in the space provided below:

1. _____

_____

_____

2. _____

_____

_____

3. _____

_____

_____

*Adapted from LEADERSHIP SKILLS FOR WOMEN by Marilyn Manning, Ph.D. and Patricia Haddock. For ordering information, see the back of this book.

TEAM PLANNING

Office teams need to understand what their goals are and who is responsible to ensure they are met. Keeping your team informed is one of your most important responsibilities as a team leader. You must also identify players outside of the team, and coordinate how your team works with them.

Planning is the key that makes teams effective and productive. Good planning eliminates confusion and duplication of effort. Without careful planning, time, effort, and money are often wasted.

Team planning includes the following:

Check your proficiency level.

I regularly:	Do Well	Could Improve
1. Interpret team goals passed down from upper management.	☐	☐
2. Convert the needs of the organization into goals and objectives for my team.	☐	☐
3. Evaluate options and select actions that contribute to reaching office goals.	☐	☐
4. Determine resources needed to meet office goals, including people, money, materials, and facilities.	☐	☐
5. Establish deadlines and timelines for all goals.	☐	☐
6. Set performance standards and measurements for goals and use during evaluations.	☐	☐

''If you are waiting for someone in higher management to tell you to build a team, you may be limiting the success of your unit and yourself. A thinking proactive manager will not wait for a directive from above. Instead, he or she will begin immediately to make a concerted effort to develop solid management skills.''

Robert B. Maddux

Author of Team Building:
An Exercise in Leadership

TEAM LEADERSHIP ACTION PLAN

The following checklist will help you identify ways to improve your skills as a team leader. Read the list and check those which are applicable:

	Do most of the time	Do sometimes	Don't do
1. I work to develop the skills of others.	☐	☐	☐
2. I use time efficiently.	☐	☐	☐
3. I am well organized.	☐	☐	☐
4. I have good listening skills.	☐	☐	☐
5. I openly express my views.	☐	☐	☐
6. I encourage others to express their views.	☐	☐	☐
7. I maintain open communication within the group.	☐	☐	☐
8. I deal constructively with conflict.	☐	☐	☐
9. I share objectives with both my team and other teams.	☐	☐	☐
10. I identify mutual needs and goals.	☐	☐	☐
11. I take product risks.	☐	☐	☐
12. I negotiate well.	☐	☐	☐

KEY RESPONSIBILITIES IN STAFFING

Hiring the right people is vital to your success as an office manager. The person you select should be evaluated carefully against an updated written job description to insure he or she has the skills and/or experience to satisfactorily fulfill the job requirements. Your hires should also display a positive attitude and solid basic communication skills.

Follow the six steps listed below to help you clarify your hiring decision.

Step One:	Review the job descriptions to ensure they are current.
Step Two:	Involve key staff people to ensure the description reflects what the job requires. Rewrite the job description based on input obtained in Steps 1 and 2.
Step Three:	Prepare a list of specific legal questions to ask the candidates.
Step Four:	Record interview responses on rating form.
Step Five:	Determine the best candidate by reviewing assessments made in rating form.
Step Six:	Ensure the candidate you select would fit into your office's environment and make a job offer.

Remember - The ultimate success of any organization is directly related to the quality of their hiring decisions.

WRITING JOB DESCRIPTIONS

A professionally developed job description includes the following five elements:*

THE PURPOSE OF THE JOB:

- What product or service is supported by the job?
- How does this job relate to other jobs in the office?
- What is the result of poor or non-performance?

WHAT THE EMPLOYEE DOES ON THE JOB:

- What are the most important job duties?
- How often are they performed?
- What kind of decisions is the person responsible for making?

HOW THE JOB IS PERFORMED:

- What are reporting relationships?
- What contacts are required inside the company?
- What contacts are required outside the company?
- What are the working conditions?

WHAT HUMAN RELATIONS OR PERSONAL SKILLS ARE NEEDED:

- What interpersonal skills are needed?
- Does the position require detail orientation, logic, reasoning, or writing skills?
- What skills are absolutely essential?
- What kind of grooming is required?

WHAT PHYSICAL QUALITIES ARE NECESSARY:

- Is physical strength required?
- Is size a factor?

Note: Physical requirements must be necessary to do the job.

---

*Adapted from QUALITY INTERVIEWING by Robert B. Maddux. For ordering information, see the back of this book.

INTERVIEWING POTENTIAL EMPLOYEES

After you have developed your job description you are ready to evaluate candidates against the criteria you have set.

Follow these tips for effective interviews.

One: Use phone interviews to obtain information and screen candidates.

Two: Decide what parts of the resumé are most important for the open position.

Three: Learn about candidate's previous job experience before offering an opportunity to interview for your open position.

Four: Hold the interview in a place where you won't be disturbed or interrupted.

Five: Establish a relaxed rapport early. Put your candidate at ease.

Six: Use open-ended questions that require more than "Yes" or "No" answers. Sample of open-ended questions are "What are your best skills for this job?" and "What was your most significant achievement on your last job?"

Seven: Use some self-appraisal questions that require candidates to evaluate themselves.

Eight: Set up hypothetical situations that require the candidate to display reasoning and/or problem-solving skills.

Nine: Thoroughly explore the candidate's experience and education.

Ten: Use action-listening techniques and repeat key items the candidate says.

Eleven: Take notes and evaluate all candidates on the same criteria.

Twelve: Request additional interviews with the most likely candidates and thoroughly check references.

Thirteen: Set up interviews with other key personnel the candidate should see before offering a job.

PROVIDE INFORMATION ABOUT THE JOB

Be prepared to discuss the following information about the job and the company:

1. A history of the company (including key products/services).

2. A general job description explaining duties and responsibilities.

3. How and when performance will be evaluated.

4. Work hours, rules, and other information about the office.

5. Compensation and benefits information.

6. The probation period, if any, required before becoming a permanent employee.

Note: Ask questions to discover job-related skills only. Questions on race, national origin, sex, religion, age, mobility impairment, or sexual preference may be considered discriminatory.*

---

*For an excellent book on this subject, order A GUIDE TO AFFIRMATIVE ACTION using the form in the back of this book.

EXAMPLE OF GOOD JOB INTERVIEW QUESTIONS

Write some specific questions for a position you plan to fill using the criteria described in the preceding pages.

Experience and Education
Example: "Describe a typical day on your current job."

1. _____

2. _____

3. _____

Intelligence and Aptitude
Example: "How do you make decisions? What process do you use?"

1. _____

2. _____

3. _____

Attitudes and Personality
Example: "What has frustrated you most in your business life?"

1. _____

2. _____

3. _____

Job Skills and Knowledge
Example: "What strengths would you bring to this job?"

1. _____

2. _____

3. _____

HIRING QUALIFIED EMPLOYEES

Because of affirmative action laws, you may be required to show that you evaluated all candidates for a position on the same basis. You must be able to demonstrate that the criteria you used in making your hiring decision were job-related. Keep carefully written documentation to avoid possible lawsuits.

If your human resources department doesn't have a standard form for evaluating job candidates, you can use one like the one shown on the facing page.

"ALL JOB CANDIDATES WILL BE EVALUATED FAIRLY."

CANDIDATE DISPOSITION FORM*

The following reasons for rejecting a candidate are valid as long as they don't apply to the person chosen for the job.

Candidate

_____ does not meet minimum job requirements.

_____ meets minimum job requirements, but is not the best qualified.

_____ has no prior related experience.

_____ has less prior experience than the person selected.

_____ cannot meet physical standards for the job.

_____ has a lower level of skills than the person selected.

_____ has less directly-related training than the person selected.

_____ cannot work the schedule required.

_____ withdrew from consideration.

Comments:

Candidate name: _____

Date: _____

Position applied for:

Job offer will (   ) will not (   ) be extended.

Job-related reason candidate selected was best qualified:

---

*Adapted from QUALITY INTERVIEWING by Robert B. Maddux. For ordering information, see the back of this book.

EFFECTIVE EMPLOYEE ORIENTATION

Thoughtful employee orientation is another important activity you will perform as an office manager. An employee's first few days on the job are critical to that employee's success. Often, an employee's attitude about the organization he or she will be working for is set on that crucial first day.

Your orientation program should include the following:

• a sincere welcome.

• an introduction to key people in the office.

• a tour of the office and building.

• a description of the fundamentals such as office hours and rules, benefits, attendance policy.

• a description of job duties and minimum job requirements.

• a description of initial training the employee will receive.

• time for the employee to familiarize himself or herself with the work area.

• a fully-equipped desk or work space.

• documents such as employment agreement, benefits handbook, company phone directory.

• a first assignment.

STEPS FOR ON-THE-JOB TRAINING*

Every training program has four steps:

Step 1. Define how the job should be done.
Step 2. Plan the training.
Step 3. Present the training.
Step 4. Evaluate the training.

On-the-job training is popular in small offices and organizations. Many office managers believe that it is one of the most effective forms of training. But on-the-job training works only if you plan it carefully.

The following should be part of your on-the-job training program.

• Construct task lists, performance standards, and training plans and lessons for each task.
• Use trainers who want to train and who understand basic training principles.
• Provide written materials such as manuals to reinforce what is taught.
• Set aside enough time to train properly.
• Provide all necessary tools and supplies to do an effective training job.
• Have a means of evaluating the training.

If any of the above items are missing from your on-the-job training programs, write action plans below to incorporate them into your training procedures.

_____

_____

_____

_____

_____

_____

*Adapted from TRAINING MANAGERS TO TRAIN by Brother Herman E. Zaccarelli, C.S.C. For ordering information, see the back of this book.

EVALUATING EMPLOYEE PERFORMANCE

The performance goals you establish, define what you want done and how you want it done. The performance appraisal process evaluates how well each employee has met these goals, based on the criteria established.

Performance appraisals have three basic functions:

1. To provide adequate feedback to each employee on his or her performance.
2. To serve as an opportunity to communicate face-to-face modifications or changes to existing performance objectives.
3. To provide data to managers or supervisors so they can evaluate an employee and judge future job assignments and compensation.

Formal performance appraisals should be conducted:

- On a regular basis that is established in writing.
- At a pre-determined time and place, free of interruptions.
- Using a document upon which performance can be summarized in writing.
- Separately from the compensation review.
- With a written follow-up outlining any action plans resulting from the performance session.

EIGHT STEPS FOR MORE EFFECTIVE PERFORMANCE APPRAISALS

| Step One: | When an employee is hired or assigned to your office, provide a written description of the behaviors and qualities required for the job. |

Step One: When an employee is hired or assigned to your office, provide a written description of the behaviors and qualities required for the job.

Step Two: Set specific goals with the employee and sign off.

Step Three: Make sure the goals are fair and reasonable so they allow you to evaluate how well the employee is doing.

Step Four: Explain that the performance review process is designed to evaluate how well goals were met and the means by which the employee achieved them.

Step Five: Obtain agreement with the employee about which behaviors and performance criteria will be evaluated.

Step Six: Set a date for the first review. Make sure you schedule the first review within any probationary period required by your office.

Step Seven: Observe the employee during the review period and document incidents of behavior that affect the employee's performance or illustrate behavior pattern.

Step Eight: Schedule the actual appraisal far enough in advance to allow employee to prepare.

APPRAISAL DISCUSSION MODELS

END RESULT OF EVALUATION	EMPLOYEE'S LIKELY FUTURE	DISCUSSION OBJECTIVE
Outstanding	Promotion	Consider opportunities
	Growth in present job	Make development plans
	Broadened assignment	Review possibility of extending responsibility
	No change in duties	How to maintain performance level
Satisfactory	Promotion	Consider possibilities
	Growth in present assignment	Make development plans
	No change in duties	How to maintain or improve performance level
Unsatisfactory	Performance correctible	Plan correction and gain commitment
	Performance uncorrectible	Review possible reassignment, or prepare for termination.

HOW ARE YOUR APPRAISALS?

WHAT CAN WELL-PLANNED PERFORMANCE APPRAISALS DO FOR YOU?*

Performance appraisals often take a low priority on an office manager's schedule. However the appraisal process in an essential communication between you and your employees and should not be ignored. There are several advantages in doing appraisals in a timely and professional manner. Check those that you agree are important:

☐ Performance appraisals provide valuable insights into the work the employee is doing and how it is being done.

☐ When you maintain good communication with employees about job expectations and results, you create opportunities for new ideas and improved methods.

☐ When you give well-planned, timely performance appraisals, employees know how they are doing and that knowledge reduces their uncertainty.

☐ When employees receive timely corrective feedback, productivity is improved.

☐ Appraisals provide an opportunity to reinforce sound work habits and publicly recognize good performance.

☐ Appraisals encourage two way communication.

☐ Learning to write and give good performance appraisals is excellent preparation for advancement and increased responsibility.

*Adapted from EFFECTIVE PERFORMANCE APPRAISALS by Robert B. Maddux. For ordering information, see the back of this book.

Office Management

HANDLING POOR PERFORMERS

You must follow a specific procedure for handling poor performers. In addition to being a sound management practice, there are legal considerations as well. The following steps need to be taken when an employee's performance is not satisfactory:

Step One: Coaching

Coaching occurs when you work with an employee to remove barriers to optimum work performance. You use coaching when an employee has a performance or attitude problem, or shows a lack of knowledge about job responsibilities.

Step Two: Verbal Notice

Verbal notice can be part of the coaching process. It requires you to say to the employee, ''Unless your attitude and/or performance improves, you will be placed on probation.'' It is essential for you to provide specifics so the employee understands precisely what his or her problems are.

Step Three: Written Notice

Written notice normally follows the verbal notice. Both you and the employee must sign the written notice and place it in the employee's file. It should tell the employee specifically what he or she must do to avoid being placed on probation. It must also tell the employee by what date corrective action must be demonstrated.

Step Four: Probation

This is a formal notification that the employee is on probation and failure to correct behaviors or performance within a specified time frame will result in termination. Make sure this step is performed in conjunction with your human resources department.

Step Five: Termination

The human resources department should review the situation (with your documentation) before you can terminate an employee. Never fire an employee on the spot or without ensuring your termination action is fully documented. Terminations will be discussed again in **Section VI: Special Problems.**

SECTION 3

ESTABLISHING MEASUREMENTS FOR THE OFFICE

"Measure. Verb. To regulate by a standard."
Webster's New Collegiate Dictionary

SETTING STANDARDS AND GOALS FOR THE OFFICE

The standards for your office are the minimum acceptable behavior you will accept from employees. For instance, an office standard may set dress criteria for public contact employees, criteria for answering the phones and correspondence, and attendance. All employees are expected to adhere to the standards of the office and the standards specific to their jobs.

Goals are the means by which you measure the performance and productivity of each employee. The performance plan is the communication process you use to let your employees know what is expected of them—what their goals are—and the performance review tells them how well they have met their goals.

STANDARDS

• must be realistic and attainable.

• should be developed with input from the employees.

• should be understood and accepted by employees.

• may refer to things such as attendance, breakage, and safety.

• are flexible and can be revised if there is a good business reason to do so.

• are normally specific and measurable.

THIS EMPLOYEE NEEDS STANDARDS

GOALS

- are statements of results you expect each employee to achieve.

- should be developed with input from the employee.

- are specific and measurable.

- describe the criteria you will use to determine if and how well the goals have been met.

- usually include a timeframe for completion, although some goals will be ongoing, especially for employees who perform routine processing functions.

- should be challenging, but achievable.

- can be replaced with new goals when the needs of the job change or a specific project is completed.

- must be consistent with office standards.

THIS EMPLOYEE NEEDS GOALS

CONTROL SYSTEMS HELP YOU ACHIEVE GOALS

Once you begin a project, you need a system to make sure it progresses according to your plan. Establish controls during the planning process and keep them simple. Then compare what happens against the control system you have established and revise the goal or process as necessary.

Some important aspects of control systems are listed below. Indicate your proficiency by checking the appropriate box.

I normally:	Do well	Need To Improve
1. Establish control elements as part of any project.	☐	☐
2. Set up time schedules and checkpoints to measure progress.	☐	☐
3. Encourage feedback from office team members throughout the project.	☐	☐
4. Evaluate deviations from project plans, and then construct new action plans as necessary.	☐	☐
5. Adjust objectives, plans, resources, or motivational factors as required to meet the organizational goals.	☐	☐
6. Communicate progress and plan changes to those who need to know.	☐	☐

Following are some thoughts about controls I want to establish:

_____

_____

_____

_____

KEEPING THE WORK FLOWING

Having a good control system allows you to keep work moving through your office.

1. BEFORE A PROJECT BEGINS:

- Define the results expected.

- List major steps.

- Set time frames.

- Make schedules.

- Decide which resources you need.

- Set checkpoints.

- Obtain understanding and acceptance of the employees who will be doing the work.

2. WHILE THE WORK IS BEING DONE:

- Require completed reports and letters.

- Follow up at specified checkpoints.

- Consider the motivation of your employees.

- Be tolerant of mistakes.

3. AFTER THE WORK IS DONE:

- Correct performance deficiencies.

- Recognize good work.

An excellent book on this topic, PROJECT MANAGEMENT may be ordered using the form in the back of this book.

RESPONSIBILITIES CHART

List the major activities for which your office has responsibility and the names of employees in charge of those activities. Identify responsibility as primary (P) or secondary (S).

Make sure each person understands his or her level of responsibility to prevent misunderstandings and blockages in work flow.

Activity	Name	Responsibility
1. _____	_____	_____
2. _____	_____	_____
3. _____	_____	_____
4. _____	_____	_____
5. _____	_____	_____
6. _____	_____	_____
7. _____	_____	_____
8. _____	_____	_____
9. _____	_____	_____
10. _____	_____	_____

IMPROVING PRODUCTIVITY*

To improve office productivity, you have to get employees excited about their jobs and contributions. Every employee wants to feel satisfied about his or her contributions. Satisfaction relates to five basic needs defined by psychologist Abraham Maslow, who observed that each person has the same basic needs and spends each day satisfying one or more of them. Maslow's hierarchy of needs are:

Need #1: The need to survive.

Need #2: The need for security.

Need #3: The need to belong.

Need #4: The need for prestige.

Need #5: The need for self-fulfillment.

Today, jobs are generally more flexible and recognize employees' needs.

The following ten qualities are what employees want most from their jobs, according to a study conducted by the Public Agenda Foundation in 1983:

Employees want:

1. To work for efficient managers.

2. To think for themselves.

3. To see the end results of their work.

4. To be assigned interesting work.

5. To be informed.

6. To be listened to.

7. To be respected.

8. To be recognized for their efforts.

9. To be challenged.

10. To have opportunities for increased skill development.

---

*Adapted from AN HONEST DAY'S WORK by Twyla Dell. For ordering information, see back of book.

IMPROVE PRODUCTIVITY BY GIVING THE TOP TEN

Rate yourself on how effectively you give your office staff the top ten qualities they want, by deciding how well you perform the following activities. Rank yourself as high, average, below average, or not at all.

Score 3 for high, 2 for average, 1 for below average, and 0 for not at all. Then total your score and compare your results with the box at the bottom of this page:

☐ I am an efficient manager.

☐ I encourage and teach employees to think for themselves.

☐ I arrange work so employees can see the end result.

☐ I assign work to make it as interesting as possible to everyone.

☐ I listen to ideas on how to do things better.

☐ I inform those who need to know about what is going on.

☐ I treat employees like professionals at all times.

☐ I recognize individuals for good work, formally and informally.

☐ I offer challenges whenever possible.

☐ I encourage skill development.

A score of 24 to 30 means you are an outstanding office manager and your work flow is probably very productive. 15 to 23 means you have potential, but can improve how you motivate employees to produce. 8 to 14 indicates that you understand the principles, but you aren't applying them to your office. You may want to enroll in a management class. A score of 0 to 7 may indicate that you need extensive training in order to improve productivity.

SECTION

LEADERSHIP AND HUMAN-RELATIONS SKILLS DEVELOPMENT

TALK · TALK · TALK · TALK

TOCK · TOCK · TOCK · TOCK

(THIS GROUP NEEDS A LEADER)

''*Leader.* Noun. A person who has commanding authority or influence.''

Webster's New Collegiate Dictionary

COMMUNICATING FOR RESULTS

Effective communication is critically important in an office. When you have strong communication skills, you are much more effective than colleagues without those skills. Good communicators know what to say and how to say it; either verbally or on paper, whether in a small office meeting, or in front of a large audience.

Effective communication skills will:

• Increase confidence, credibility, and competence.

• Reduce misunderstandings and confusion.

• Save time for everyone.

• Help you better defend your positions on project and budget matters.

Developing effective oral and written communication skills is essential for anyone in a managerial job. Those same skills are equally valuable at home or in activities such as PTA, church, political, and volunteer organizations, and memberships in professional associations.

When you know how to communicate effectively, you are able to:

• Develop and express ideas and opinions.

• Listen for and accurately repeat what others say.

• Choose the correct words for your listener and appropriately color those words with feelings.

LEARNING TO LISTEN

Effective listening means that you get the most meaning from what you hear. Good listening skills are important if you plan to be a success as office manager. A good listener is able to reduce mistakes and misunderstandings. In an office, this usually leads to savings of time and money.

The following steps will help improve your listening skills:

1. Let speakers finish what they are saying before responding.

2. Concentrate on what the speaker is saying.

3. Try to eliminate outside distractions during the conversation.

4. Study the speaker's body language and tone as well as what is said.

5. Pace your responses with those of the speaker, repeating words they use, matching body language or leading them to change body language by changing your own.

6. Nod your head occasionally to show you are listening.

7. Paraphrase what the speaker said to make sure you heard it properly and understood the meaning of his or her message.

TEST THE EFFECTIVENESS OF YOUR COMMUNICATIONS

Check the box that corresponds to how often you perform these effective communication strategies.

	Usually	Often	Never
1. Do you check grammer and punctuation to insure it is 100% correct before you mail any correspondence?	☐	☐	☐
2. Do you check to make sure you have chosen suitable words for your audience?	☐	☐	☐
3. When you take messages, do you make sure you have all essential information and write it down?	☐	☐	☐
4. Do you ask questions if you're not sure of the facts?	☐	☐	☐
5. Do you repeat the theme of the message to make sure you understand it correctly?	☐	☐	☐
6. Do you speak clearly and concisely?	☐	☐	☐
7. Do you use only words you understand?	☐	☐	☐
8. Do you ask for questions to make sure others understand you?	☐	☐	☐
9. Do you present your points in a friendly, rational manner, and do your best to avoid arguing?	☐	☐	☐
10. Do you concentrate on what others are saying when they are speaking to you?	☐	☐	☐

NOW YOU TRY IT!

For any "Often" or "Never" answers you checked on the facing page, write your plan for improving to "Always".

1. _____

_____

_____

2. _____

_____

_____

3. _____

_____

_____

4. _____

_____

_____

5. _____

_____

_____

6. _____

_____

_____

7. _____

_____

_____

GIVING FEEDBACK

Good communication is especially important in an office environment. It requires clear thinking and practice. It means you state your thoughts and feelings so the listener will know exactly what you mean.

Make your words meaningful. Choose the best words to let your listener know how you feel.

Select the best environment in which to communicate. Make sure the timing is right and, as much as possible, eliminate distractions. Know what you want to say, why you want to say it, and what results you want to achieve. Present your points in a calm, clear, and rational way.

Concentration is your strongest listening skill. Repeat what you believe the person said, to confirm your interpretation. Your desire to establish communication will help dissolve any barriers to open discussion.

HOW NOT TO GIVE FEEDBACK

IT'S WHAT YOU DON'T SAY THAT COUNTS*

Your attitude is your most effective communication strategy. Your attitude communicates even more than your words.

Your attitude sets the pace for the office. People tend to mirror each other; and employees especially tend to mirror managers. If your attitude is positive and dynamic, people you work with will tend to reflect your attitude by becoming more positive and dynamic. If, however, you complain and play the victim, you will find yourself surrounded by reflections of yourself.

Your attitude will also affect your department's productivity. When you develop good relationships with employees and make them feel like part of a team, they will respond by wanting to meet or exceed departmental goals.

No one can be upbeat all the time. Sometimes personal problems, health problems, and people problems seem to conspire to erode our positive feelings and attitudes.

Follow some tips to help keep your attitude positive, especially during those ''down'' times:*

- Engage in a regular exercise program.

- Inject humor into your life and your workplace.

- Break major goals into smaller, more easily attainable ones.

- Take frequent, short time-outs during the day for renewal.

- Balance work and leisure more effectively.

- Try volunteering to add prespective and depth to your life.

- Keep yourself looking professional.

- Find someone you trust as a role model, confidant, and sounding board.

---

*From *ATTITUDE: YOUR MOST PRICELESS POSSESSION* by Elwood N. Chapman.
  See back of this book for ordering information.

DEALING WITH DIFFICULT PEOPLE

Difficult people can be negative, irritating, and too often, seemingly impossible to deal with. They can be employees, customers, peers, and managers. And they create stress for everyone around them.

When you can assess the person's behavior and really listen to what is said, you can more effectively handle a difficult personality.

Following are seven basic types of difficult people:

1. **ATTACKERS:** Attackers charge and need room and time to blow off steam. Get them into a private area, address them by name and listen to their position. Don't argue or get in a shouting match; ask them to calm down and present your response in a firm, calm way.

2. **EGOTISTS:** Egotists also come on strong, but unlike attackers, they often act like subject experts. Respect their knowledge and ask questions, but don't allow them to "take over."

3. **SNEAKS:** Sneaks often use sarcasm. Your best defense is to expose them with direct questions about what bothers them. They often retreat if directly queried about what their sarcasm really means.

4. **VICTIMS:** Victims act powerless and defeated, and often whine. Ask them for suggestions to improve the situation. Logically refute their negative comments with facts.

5. **NEGATORS:** Negators are usually suspicious of those in authority and believe that their opinion is the only legitimate one. Let negators use all their negative "ammunition" before focusing on real solutions.

6. **SUPER-AGREEABLE PEOPLE:** Super-agreeable people want to be liked and offer to do whatever you want them to do. They overcommit themselves and often disappoint and frustrate others. Monitor what they volunteer to do to make sure they aren't overworked. Disassociate actions from their sense of self-worth.

7. **UNRESPONSIVE PEOPLE:** Unresponsive people are withdrawn and it is seemingly impossible to gain a positive commitment from them. Try using more open-ended, indirect questions and wait for them to respond. Resist the urge to finish sentences for them. Give them tasks that require reports at regular intervals.

MANAGING CONFLICT IN THE OFFICE*

Even if everyone has agreed on a goal, disagreements can occur.

Here are seven suggestions for resolving conflict:

1. Schedule a meeting with the other person to discuss the situation.

2. When you meet, acknowledge there is a conflict.

3. Use "I" statements to avoid accusations. ("I feel we are not together on the office fax machine policy, what do you think?"). Make sure the other person uses "I" statements, too.

4. Ask questions that require the other person to talk about the situation. Good questions start with "Would you share your feelings about the way office fax machine scheduling is being handlled?"

5. Repeat what you are being told. "You're telling me that we need a scheduling sheet for the fax?" is a good way to confirm that you understand what you are hearing.

6. State what each of you want as an outcome.

7. Agree to work toward a resolution and schedule a meeting to follow-up on the situation.

---

*Adapted from LEADERSHIP SKILLS FOR WOMEN by Marilyn Manning, Ph.D. and P.A. Haddock. See back of this book for ordering information.

RULES TO PREVENT CONFLICT FROM ESCALATING

STUDY THE PROBLEM

DO MORE LISTENING THAN TALKING

SEE THE TOTAL SITUATION

ASK QUESTIONS TO FIND OUT THE REAL MEANING OF WORDS

AVOID MAKING MORAL JUDGEMENTS

TRY TO EMPHATHIZE

PUT PROBLEMS ON THE BACK-BURNER IF SOLUTIONS AREN'T OBVIOUS

*WATCH OUT FOR PITFALLS
AS YOU PREPARE!*

PITFALLS IN CONFLICT MANAGEMENT

DO YOU AVOID GIVING NEGATIVE FEEDBACK? Yes ☐ No ☐

If you answered "Yes", you may be encouraging office conflicts. Problems don't go away by avoiding them. They tend to escalate.

Hone your communication skills so that you can frame criticism as positively as possible to motivate the person to change his or her behavior.

DO YOU REACT WITH ANGER WHEN
A CONFLICT ARISES? Yes ☐ No ☐

Anger can be a two-edged sword. Used sparingly and in drastic circumstances, it can be most effective. Used often and indiscriminately, it will damage your reputation and lose you the respect of others.

Control your anger by taking deep breaths, going for a walk, or talking it out with a confidante. If you lose your temper and act inappropriately, be prepared to apologize for your behavior, not your feelings of anger.

If you are dealing with an angry employee, customer, or peer, allow the person to blow off steam, but within reason.

Firmly and immediately stop any tirade or abuse.

DO YOU BLAME OTHERS FOR THEIR PROBLEMS? Yes ☐ No ☐

When you place blame, you put your attention in the wrong place. Blame wastes time and does not address the real problem or its solution. When you place blame on someone, you abdicate authority and control.

Instead of playing blame games, assess the situation and define solutions. Make sure people are accountable for their actions and the results of their actions and take corrective action to improve performance, but don't place blame.

MANAGING CHANGE

Computers. Electronic advances. Reorganizations. Downsizing.

It all means change.

In the words of Machiavelli, ''There is nothing more difficult to take in hand, more perilous to conduct, or more uncertain in its success, than to take the lead in introducing a new order of things.''

Everywhere an office manager looks, she or he finds change occurring.

Employees *like* business as usual. They feel secure with the familiar. Often, change creates some basic fears, such as loss of control, uncertainty, surprise, and having to take on more work. Change is often greeted with resistance, excuses, and reasons for why it won't work. But change can offer opportunity.

Change is necessary to survival. Organization must change to remain competitive. The playing field is never level for long, and office managers must take a lead in coping with and helping their employees through change.

*SUCCESSFUL CHANGE IS BUILT
IN SMALL STEPS*

CHANGE ACTION SHEET

The following worksheet will help you implement change effectively.

WHO initiated the change?

WHAT is the nature of the change?

WHAT steps need to be taken to accomplish the change?

WHAT follow-up actions will be required?

WHO will be the primary changemaker?

WHO needs to be involved in the change process?

WHO needs to be informed of the change?

WHAT personnel problems might the change create?

HOW will I inform my office about the change?

HOW will others be affected?

HOW will I know I have been successful in helping implement the change?

WHAT details about the change need to be communicated?

WHEN will each step be completed?

WHEN can I expect the change to be in place?

Note: for three excellent books on managing change order MANAGING PERSONAL CHANGE: MANAGING ORGANIZATIONAL CHANGE and UNDERSTANDING ORGANIZATIONAL CHANGE using the form in the back of this book.

HONING NEGOTIATION SKILLS

A good manager knows how to set up win-win situations and keep everyone moving toward the office's goals. But learning this skill takes time and practice. It takes the ability to compromise and negotiate.

- Always know what your high and low expectations are.

- Tackle the easy issues first.

- Be prepared to change your mind.

- Leave yourself a way out.

- Allow time to identify your options.

- Make sure each party feels as if something has been gained.

- Use persuasion, not intimidation.

- Be patient.

- Hold your temper.

- Listen.

- Resolve any conflicts that arise.

NEVER MAKE PROMISES YOU CAN'T KEEP.

NEVER LIE.

NEVER ASSUME ANYTHING.

BUILDING WIN-WIN SITUATIONS*

Negotiating is an important skill, especially in a busy office.

The following six steps are common to most successful negotiations. Keep them in mind before you begin your next negotiation.

Step One: Get to know the party you will be negotiating with. Keep your initial interactions friendly, relaxed, and businesslike.

Step Two: Be prepared to share your goals and objectives with the other party, and expect to learn their goals and objectives. The atmosphere should be cooperative and trusting.

Step Three: Raise specific issues to start the process. Study all issues before negotiations begin to see where issues can be split or combined. Obtain a consensus about spliting or combining issues and begin dealing with them one by one.

Step Four: Express areas of agreement or conflict.

Step Five: Reassess your position and decide what level of compromise is acceptable.

Step Six: The final step is to affirm agreements and put them in writing.

*From SUCCESSFUL NEGOTIATION by Robert B. Maddux. See ordering information at back of book.

NEGOTIATING QUESTIONNAIRE

1. With which people at your office are you most likely to negotiate with?

2. With which people outside your office are you most likely to negotiate?

3. With whom do you find it easiest to negotiate?

4. Are there people you cannot negotiate with? Why?

5. What areas of your job are you most likely to negotiate?

6. What subjects do you find it easiest to negotiate?

7. What areas of your job do you feel are not negotiable? Why?

TACTICAL PLANNING FOR OFFICE NEGOTIATIONS

1. What are the goals, issues, problems, targets that need negotiating?

2. What is the timing?

3. Do you need to offer an inspection? product? facility? service? To what extent?

4. What party is involved? Are other parties likely to be involved?

5. Who has the authority to make the decisions for your office? For the other party?

6. How much flexibility do you have, i.e., how much are you willing to spend? Sell? What concessions are you willing to make? Ask for?

7. What is your opening offer? Question? What response strategies do you have that will move you closer to your goals?

8. What is your relationship to the party with whom you are negotiating?

9. What do you want your relationship to be after negotiations end?

CONDUCTING EFFECTIVE MEETINGS

Office managers spend roughly 20 percent of their time at meetings. Meetings are one of the most important ways to communicate within an office environment.

To make the most of office meetings, follow these steps:

One: Contact attendees before the actual meeting to obtain support for ideas and build the foundations you will need to defend your ideas and suggestions.

Two: Assuming you conduct the meeting, identify who will make formal presentations.

Three: Determine what will be discussed and distribute an agenda prior to the meeting, (at least a day in advance if possible).

Four: State how long the meeting will last and control the time of each speaker to insure it ends on time.

Five: Prepare charts or reports before the meeting and make sure needed equipment such as overhead projectors are in working order before attendees arrive.

Six: Start the meeting promptly at the announced time.

Seven: Control the meeting. Keep discussions and attendees on track.

Eight: Summarize what action was decided and provide a written follow-up assigning specific responsibilities and timelines for those involved.

Nine: Evaluate the effectiveness of the meeting and how it can be improved.

For an excellent book on meetings, order EFFECTIVE MEETING SKILLS by Marion E. Haynes. See the back of this book for ordering information.

DECISION-MAKING IN THE OFFICE

1. DEFINE THE SITUATION/PROBLEM

    Are there divided loyalties?
    Is it an ethical or values dilemma?

2. GATHER THE FACTS

    Do you have the information you need?
    Is it necessary to involve other parties?

3. TEST THE OPTIONS

    Is the option legal?
    Is it beneficial?
    What are short-term vs. long-term consequences?
    Do the benefits outweigh any potential harm?
    Is it right?
    How will it be perceived by others?
    Could it embarrass your organization?

4. MAKE YOUR DECISION

5. SHARE YOUR DECISION WITH THOSE DIRECTLY INVOLVED

SECTION 5

THE IMPORTANCE OF GOOD CUSTOMER RELATIONS

WELL YES, MADAME... BUT WE **DID** REMOVE THE STAIN.

"*Customer.* Noun. One that purchases, usually systematically or frequently, a commodity or service."

Webster's New Collegiate Dictionary

UNDERSTANDING CUSTOMER NEEDS*

Most offices are designed to support customers or clients, whether they are external, or internal (i.e. other departments). In any case, good customer relation skills are essential. Read the following to gain a better understanding of what customers want or need:

It is important for you to know!

What your customers want

What your customers need

What your customers think

What your customers feel

Whether your customers are satisfied

Whether your customers will return

Following is a list of common human needs. Check those that reflect the needs of your customers, clients, or guests.

_____ 1. The need to feel welcome.

_____ 2. The need for timely service.

_____ 3. The need for quality, reliable products.

_____ 4. The need to be understood.

_____ 5. The need to feel comfortable.

_____ 6. The need to receive help or assistance.

_____ 7. The need to feel important.

_____ 8. The need to be appreciated.

_____ 9. The need to be recognized or remembered.

_____ 10. The need for respect.

---

*Adapted from QUALITY CUSTOMER SERVICE by William B. Martin.
 See back of book for ordering information.

CREATING A CUSTOMER-FIRST ENVIRONMENT

Step 1: Encourage the office staff to develop a genuine interest in customers or co-workers and their well-being.

Step 2: Develop an atmosphere of openness, honesty, and integrity.

Step 3: Develop a sense of mutual respect between employees and customers.

Step 4: Acknowledge that customers have a right to their own decision.

Step 5: Do not tolerate office employees coercing, pressuring, controlling, or manipulating customers.

HANDLING CUSTOMER COMPLAINTS

There are three main styles to deal with angry customers. They are:

1. **PASSIVE RESPONSE:** The customer rants and raves while a member of your office staff apologizes profusely and accepts the blame for what went wrong.

PASSIVE

2. **AGGRESSIVE RESPONSE:** Your employee rants and raves and refuses to take responsibility for what happened.

AGGRESSIVE

3. **ASSERTIVE RESPONSE:** Your employee listens carefully in order to understand the problem, and then responds supportively and acknowledges how the customer feels without becoming a doormat or responding in kind.

ASSERTIVE

The assertive response is the most effective and the one you want to encourage in your employees. The following six steps can help your staff develop an asssertive response to customer complaints:

One: Listen to the complaint.

Two: Repeat the complaint and obtain acknowledgment that you heard it correctly.

Three: Apologize if appropriate.

Four: Acknowledge the person's feelings.

Five: Explain what action you will take to correct the problem.

Six: Thank the person for bringing the problem to your attention.

COMPLAINT-SOLVING EXERCISE

Identify what is wrong with each response and describe what it should be:

Customer: "Why must I pay a $10 returned check fee because someone gave me a bad check and my account went overdrawn? It's not my fault!"

Employee: "Because those are the rules."

Your response:

(Start by acknowledging the customer's feelings: "I can understand your frustration. It probably doesn't seem fair.")

Customer: "Why can't Jane wait on me?"

Employee: "Jane no longer works in this department."

Your response:

(State the facts so that the customer agrees with you: "Jane was so outstanding in her job, you'll be pleased to know that she was promoted. She thought you'd enjoy working with Susan, whom she personally trained.")

Customer: "Why are your prices higher than your competitors?"

Employee: "I don't think they are high."

Your response:

(Try to satisfy the customer: "Prices can vary according to services provided. Let's look at the specific services you need.")

(Continued next page)

COMPLAINT SOLVING EXERCISE
(Continued)

Customer: "You were supposed to come this morning and I've been waiting all day!"

Employee: "Our truck broke down and we're behind schedule."

Your response:

(Acknowledge the customer's feelings: "I'm sorry you were inconvenienced. It's so frustrating when an unexpected delay happens.")

Customer: "Why did you deny my claim? My doctor ordered this?"

Employee: "It's not covered under your contract."

Your response:

(Acknowledge the customer's frustration and anger: "You must feel upset about this. Let me clarify a few points about your coverage.")

Customer: "I bought this at one of your stores. Can I return it here?"

Employee: "No."

Your response:

(Try to help the customer: "We don't carry the same stock at each store. Let me check with our central office about how to best handle this.")

OFFICE PARTIES

Many a marriage and more than a few careers have been ruined because of an office party. Office social functions can work for you or against you.

A social gathering sponsored by the office offers a way of saying ''Thanks'' to your staff, associates, and/or customers. It also offers the chance to get to know people in a more relaxed atmosphere and see each other as rounded human beings, not just the data input operator or the company's biggest customer. It also provides a way of commemorating significant events such as performance milestones, anniversaries, retirements, and/or promotions.

Here are some rules for office parties:

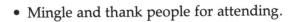

- Clearly define a beginning and ending time for the party and enforce them.

- Choose an off-site location if alcoholic beverages are to be served. Monitor the amount of alcohol to be served and *never* allow anyone to leave an office party in an impaired way if he or she is driving!

- Make sure plenty of alternative non-alcoholic beverages are available for non-drinkers.

- Serve appetizers or other food to help offset the effects of alcohol.

- Have a program (no matter how informal) to let attendees know the purpose of the party and recognize any special person/or achievement.

- Make sure someone assumes responsibility to act as host or hostess.

- Mingle and thank people for attending.

SECTION 6

SPECIAL
PROBLEMS

"Problem. Noun. A question raised for inquiry, consideration, or solution."

Webster's New Collegiate Dictionary

SPECIAL PROBLEMS

As office manager you will have to deal with:

- **Equal Employment Opportunity**

- **Terminating Employees**

- **Ethics in the Workplace**

BEWARE OF PITFALLS AS
YOU BECAME INVOLVED IN THESE AREAS

EQUAL EMPLOYMENT OPPORTUNITY

You must establish and maintain an office climate that ensures that all employees, vendors, and customers are treated fairly and are evaluated on the basis of their qualifications. Decisions must be weighed against objective criteria and agreement with federal, state, and local laws.

Test your knowledge of affirmative action policy and laws by answering True or False to the following questions:

1. T   F   Affirmative Action and Equal Employment Opportunity laws apply only to those doing business with the government.

2. T   F   Affirmative Action is a quota system to insure employment for a certain number of women and minorities.

3. T   F   Minority and female applicants should not be hired or promoted if they don't have the qualifications necessary to perform the job.

4. T   F   During an interview, a female applicant mentions she is divorced and has two small children. She qualifies for the position, but you are concerned about how the children will be cared for. In addition you suspect she will be absent when the children are ill. These concerns will support a decision not to hire her.

5. T   F   You must layoff one employee. You should select the one with the poorest performance record regardless of age, race, religion, sex, handicap, or veterans status.

6. T   F   A permanently disabled applicant who is confined to a wheel chair is technically qualified for a position in your data processing department. Hiring him would mean installing a ramp and modifying bathroom facilities for him. You should do it.

7. T   F   As an employer, you are obligated to pay men and women equally for the job they perform regardless of any other income they may receive.

8. T   F   Employees who tell ethnic jokes in their place of employment add to morale and good will and are therefore doing no harm.

9. T   F   It is perfectly legal to ask applicants if they have ever been arrested.

10. T   F   Any applicant or current employee has the right to bring charges against an employer for discrimination at any time.

(Answers—next page)

ANSWERS:
EQUAL EMPLOYMENT
OPPORTUNITY QUIZ

Answers:

1. False. If you are not sure of your status, copies of local, state, and federal laws can be obtained from the appropriate government agencies.

2. False. Affirmative Action means going beyond compliance with the law and includes taking assertive steps to insure equal representation of women and minorities at all levels within an organization.

3. True. Nothing in the Equal Opportunity Employment laws requires the hiring or promotion of unqualified people.

4. False. You should be concerned only with her qualifications for the job. The other concerns are assumptions without basis in fact.

5. True. Performance is the name of the game.

6. True. The regulations require "reasonable accommodation" which is determined partly on the basis of "financial cost and expenses" and "business necessity."

7. True. Equal pay for equal work has nothing to do with outside income.

8. False. Such behavior may be demoralizing, embarrassing and even threatening to some employees. Managers who permit or engage in this practice create a negative work climate for employees.

9. False. Violates federal, state and many city laws. This question has been ruled inappropriate by most compliance agencies. Statistics indicate minorities have been arrested (but not necessarily convicted) more than non-minorities, therefore, it could have an adverse impact on minority applicants.

10 True. The Equal Employment Opportunity Act of 1972 enabled the Equal Employment Opportunity Commission (EEOC) to enforce Title VII in covered organizations through court action.

---

*Adapted from GUIDE TO AFFIRMATIVE ACTION by Pamela J. Conrad and Robert B Maddux. See back of book for ordering information.

TERMINATING EMPLOYEES

Why things go wrong:

When you make hiring decisions there should be a good fit between the job and the employee. But even the best interviewers hire people who don't work out. Here are some reasons why that happens.

A candidate was able to mask or defuse certain problems by being an adept interviewee.

The employee experienced changes in personal or professional goals while on the job that affected his or her fit with the job.

Situational considerations such as bad chemistry between co-workers or changing responsibilities did not meet with an employee's expectations.

List other reasons why an employee may not work out:

1.

2.

3.

TERMINATION

Guidelines For Terminating Employees

1. Focus only on the relevant job behaviors and documented performance measurements when conducting the final termination interview.

2. Offer some constructive comments, but be sure that they do not imply you would rehire the person or rescind the termination.

3. Conduct the termination interview in a quiet, private place where you will not be interrupted.

4. Terminate the employee early in the week so there can be some adjustment to the reality by the weekend.

5. Document everything.

6. Prior to the termination interview work with your human resources department. Ensure you are clear about the provisions of the termination. Is the employee to pack up and leave that day? Can she or he stay for a period of days? Will there be any outplacement help offered? What are the provisions for benefit continuation and for what period of time?

7. Make sure all of the above is in writing and given to the employee to review and sign.

8. At the time of termination, get any necessary releases from legal action or any agreement about non-disclosure that may be required.

ETHICS IN THE WORKPLACE

As an office manager, you are expected to understand, interpret, and manage the corporate value system.

Most businesses face violations of ethical standards by employees, associates, or customers. As a manager, you are confronted with ethical problems involving employee theft, lying, and cheating. You must also make sure your decisions reflect your ethical standards of conduct, and are not made solely for expedience, favoritism, or personal preference. Your code of ethics helps establish ethical conduct between management and employees, and the company and its customers and vendors.

According to Thomas Murphy, retired chairman of General Motors, the ''temptation is often great to bend the rules, but management must stand strong in its convictions. I have never made a decision contrary to my moral and religious upbringing.''

There are five steps for establishing an ethical workplace.

Step One: State your corporate values and make sure all of your employees understand them and how they apply to daily activities.

Step Two: Make sure your word is your bond. Act with integrity and expect employees and associates to do so as well.

Step Three: Express your appreciation. Demonstrations of gratitude strengthen the ethical foundation of your office and encourage ethical behavior from others.

Step Four: Make others successful.

Step Five: Make sure all your decisions reflect your ethical standards and values.

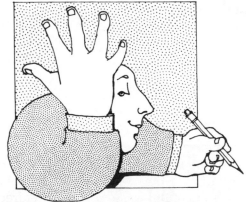

REMEMBER THESE FIVE

ETHICS EXERCISES

Rotary International offers one of the simplest ethical systems of any organization or business. It applies The Four-Step Test to every situation:

- Is it the truth?

- Is it fair to all concerned?

- Will it build good will and better friendships?

- Will it be beneficial to all concerned?

Here's how The Four-Step Test can apply to specific situations.

1. Your office hires an employee who previously worked for the competition. During a debriefing, the new employee quotes from memory cost figures on a current bid made by his former employer.

   Can you use the information?

   (This is unethical behavior on the part of the new employee. You cannot use the information.)

2. Joe, one of your employees sits behind two employees from a competitor on a plane. Unaware of Joe, the employees loudly discuss plans to announce a new competitive product. Joe overhears and takes a few notes.

   Can Joe give you the information? Can you use it?

   (It is not unethical for Joe to repeat what he heard as he did not solicit the information. However, if it violates Joe's personal value system it should not be repeated.)

3. You are on the bus and notice that someone who works for a competitor has left behind a document that may affect a project your office is bidding on.

   Should you read the document and use the information?

> (No. The material could be proprietary written information. It should not be read. It should be mailed back to the organization to which it belongs.)

PROFESSIONAL DEVELOPMENT REVIEW

Answer the following questions as honestly as possible. Use them to help you apply what you have learned from this book.

1. What are your personal goals?

2. What are your professional office goals?

3. What skills have you recently learned to help you achieve both personal and office goals?
   Personal:

   Office:

4. What training have you taken that can make you a more professional office manager?

5. What training have you given your employees to help your office be a more productive?

6. What training are you planning over the next year?

7. How will it contribute to your goals?

8. How do you plan to apply to your office what you have learned from this book?

ABOUT THE AUTHORS

Marilyn Manning, Ph.D is an internationally recognized speaker, seminar leader and author. She is president of her own management consulting firm in Mountain View, California, and recently served as president of the world's largest chapter of the National Speakers Association. In addition to office management topics, her presentations include ''Building High-Productivity Teams,'' ''Managing Conflict and Stress,'' and ''Professional Excellence.'' Her clients include General Electric, AT&T, General Motors, Apple Computer, United Airlines, and Stanford University Hospital among many others. Dr. Manning has authored several books and produced a number of best-selling audio tapes. For more information about Dr. Manning's presentations, write to her at 945 Mountain View Avenue, Mountain View, CA, 94040, or call 415-965-3663.

Patricia Haddock is a former assistant vice president of communications for a major California bank. She is a communications consultant specializing in corporate publications, speechwriting, and promotional material. Her corporate clients include Industrial Indemnity, and the Just Say No Foundation among others. She has written several juvenile books and more than 300 magazine articles on self-improvement and business topics. She is a member of the American Society of Journalists and Authors, The Authors Guild, and Associated Business Writers of America. She can be reached at #1 Hallidie Plaza, Suite 701, San Francisco, CA, 94102, or call 415-863-3917.

YOUR FEEDBACK IS IMPORTANT

This book is the result of feedback from hundreds of people in training workshops and seminars. Feedback is vital to be of continuing value. For this reason, please take a moment and note three positives and three negatives for you in reading this book.

POSITIVES

1.

2.

3.

NEGATIVES

1.

2.

3.

Thank you for your input.

Please mail to:
> Marilyn Manning
> Managing The Office
> c/o Crisp Publications, Inc.
> 95 First Street
> Los Altos, CA 94022

NOTES

FOR OTHER FIFTY-MINUTE SELF-STUDY BOOKS
SEE ORDER FORM AT THE BACK OF THE BOOK.

NOTES

FOR OTHER FIFTY-MINUTE SELF-STUDY BOOKS
SEE ORDER FORM AT THE BACK OF THE BOOK.

NOTES

FOR OTHER FIFTY-MINUTE SELF-STUDY BOOKS
SEE ORDER FORM AT THE BACK OF THE BOOK.

ORDER FORM
THE FIFTY-MINUTE SERIES

Quantity	Title	Code #	Price	Amount
	MANAGEMENT TRAINING			
	Self-Managing Teams	00-0	$7.95	
	Delegating for Results	008-6	$7.95	
	Successful Negotiation — Revised	09-2	$7.95	
	Increasing Employee Productivity	10-8	$7.95	
	Personal Performance Contracts — Revised	12-2	$7.95	
	Team Building — Revised	16-5	$7.95	
	Effective Meeting Skills	33-5	$7.95	
	An Honest Day's Work: Motivating Employees	39-4	$7.95	
	Managing Disagreement Constructively	41-6	$7.95	
	Learning To Lead	43-4	$7.95	
	The Fifty-Minute Supervisor — 2/e	58-0	$7.95	
	Leadership Skills for Women	62-9	$7.95	
	Coaching & Counseling	68-8	$7.95	
	Ethics in Business	69-6	$7.95	
	Understanding Organizational Change	71-8	$7.95	
	Project Management	75-0	$7.95	
	Risk Taking	076-9	$7.95	
	Managing Organizational Change	80-7	$7.95	
	Working Together in a Multi-Cultural Organization	85-8	$7.95	
	Selecting And Working With Consultants	87-4	$7.95	
	Empowerment	096-5	$7.95	
	Managing for Commitment	099-X	$7.95	
	Rate Your Skills as a Manager	101-5	$7.95	
	PERSONNEL/HUMAN RESOURCES			
	Your First Thirty Days: A Professional Image in a New Job	003-5	$7.95	
	Office Management: A Guide to Productivity	005-1	$7.95	
	Men and Women: Partners at Work	009-4	$7.95	
	Effective Performance Appraisals — Revised	11-4	$7.95	
	Quality Interviewing — Revised	13-0	$7.95	
	Personal Counseling	14-9	$7.95	
	Giving and Receiving Criticism	023-X	$7.95	
	Attacking Absenteeism	042-6	$7.95	
	New Employee Orientation	46-7	$7.95	
	Professional Excellence for Secretaries	52-1	$7.95	
	Guide to Affirmative Action	54-8	$7.95	
	Writing a Human Resources Manual	70-X	$7.95	
	Downsizing Without Disaster	081-7	$7.95	
	Winning at Human Relations	86-6	$7.95	
	High Performance Hiring	088-4	$7.95	
	COMMUNICATIONS			
	Technical Writing in the Corporate World	004-3	$7.95	
	Effective Presentation Skills	24-6	$7.95	
	Better Business Writing — Revised	25-4	$7.95	

Quantity	Title	Code #	Price	Amount
	COMMUNICATIONS (continued)			
	The Business of Listening	34-3	$7.95	
	Writing Fitness	35-1	$7.95	
	The Art of Communicating	45-9	$7.95	
	Technical Presentation Skills	55-6	$7.95	
	Making Humor Work	61-0	$7.95	
	50 One Minute Tips to Better Communication	071-X	$7.95	
	Speed-Reading in Business	78-5	$7.95	
	Influencing Others	84-X	$7.95	
	PERSONAL IMPROVEMENT			
	Attitude: Your Most Priceless Possession — Revised	011-6	$7.95	
	Personal Time Management	22-X	$7.95	
	Successful Self-Management	26-2	$7.95	
	Business Etiquette And Professionalism	32-9	$7.95	
	Balancing Home & Career — Revised	35-3	$7.95	
	Developing Positive Assertiveness	38-6	$7.95	
	The Telephone and Time Management	53-X	$7.95	
	Memory Skills in Business	56-4	$7.95	
	Developing Self-Esteem	66-1	$7.95	
	Managing Personal Change	74-2	$7.95	
	Finding Your Purpose	072-8	$7.95	
	Concentration!	073-6	$7.95	
	Plan Your Work/Work Your Plan!	078-7	$7.95	
	Stop Procrastinating: Get To Work!	88-2	$7.95	
	12 Steps to Self-Improvement	102-3	$7.95	
	CREATIVITY			
	Systematic Problem Solving & Decision Making	63-7	$7.95	
	Creativity in Business	67-X	$7.95	
	Intuitive Decision Making	098-1	$7.95	
	TRAINING			
	Training Managers to Train	43-2	$7.95	
	Visual Aids in Business	77-7	$7.95	
	Developing Instructional Design	076-0	$7.95	
	Training Methods That Work	082-5	$7.95	
	WELLNESS			
	Mental Fitness: A Guide to Emotional Health	15-7	$7.95	
	Wellness in the Workplace	020-5	$7.95	
	Personal Wellness	21-3	$7.95	
	Preventing Job Burnout	23-8	$7.95	
	Job Performance and Chemical Dependency	27-0	$7.95	
	Overcoming Anxiety	29-9	$7.95	
	Productivity at the Workstation	41-8	$7.95	
	Healthy Strategies for Working Women	079-5	$7.95	
	CUSTOMER SERVICE/SALES TRAINING			
	Sales Training Basics — Revised	02-5	$7.95	
	Restaurant Server's Guide — Revised	08-4	$7.95	
	Effective Sales Management	31-0	$7.95	

Quantity	Title	Code #	Price	Amount
	CUSTOMER SERVICE/SALES TRAINING (continued)			
	Professional Selling	42-4	$7.95	
	Telemarketing Basics	60-2	$7.95	
	Telephone Courtesy & Customer Service — Revised	64-7	$7.95	
	Calming Upset Customers	65-3	$7.95	
	Quality at Work	72-6	$7.95	
	Managing Quality Customer Service	83-1	$7.95	
	Customer Satisfaction — Revised	84-1	$7.95	
	Quality Customer Service — Revised	95-5	$7.95	
	SMALL BUSINESS/FINANCIAL PLANNING			
	Consulting for Success	006-X	$7.95	
	Understanding Financial Statements	22-1	$7.95	
	Marketing Your Consulting or Professional Services	40-8	$7.95	
	Starting Your New Business	44-0	$7.95	
	Direct Mail Magic	075-2	$7.95	
	Credits & Collections	080-9	$7.95	
	Publicity Power	82-3	$7.95	
	Writing & Implementing Your Marketing Plan	083-3	$7.95	
	Personal Financial Fitness — Revised	89-0	$7.95	
	Financial Planning With Employee Benefits	90-4	$7.95	
	ADULT LITERACY/BASIC LEARNING			
	Returning to Learning: Getting Your G.E.D.	02-7	$7.95	
	Study Skills Strategies — Revised	05-X	$7.95	
	The College Experience	07-8	$7.95	
	Basic Business Math	24-8	$7.95	
	Becoming an Effective Tutor	28-0	$7.95	
	Reading Improvement	086-8	$7.95	
	Introduction to Microcomputers	087-6	$7.95	
	Clear Writing	094-9	$7.95	
	Building Blocks of Business Writing	095-7	$7.95	
	Language, Customs & Protocol	097-3	$7.95	
	CAREER BUILDING			
	Career Discovery	07-6	$7.95	
	Effective Networking	30-2	$7.95	
	Preparing for Your Interview	33-7	$7.95	
	Plan B: Protecting Your Career	48-3	$7.95	
	I Got The Job!	59-9	$7.95	
	Job Search That Works	105-8	$7.95	

	Amount
Total Books	
Less Discount	
Total	
California Tax (California residents add 7%)	
Shipping	
TOTAL	

☐ Please send me a free Video Catalog.   ☐ Please add my name to your mailing list.

 ☐ Mastercard   VISA ☐ VISA   AMERICAN EXPRESS ☐ AMEX   Exp. Date _____

Account No. _____   Name (as appears on card) _____

Ship to: _____   Bill to: _____

_____   _____

_____   _____

_____   _____

Phone number: _____   P.O. #: _____

**All orders of less than $25.00 must be prepaid. Bill to orders require a company P.O.#.
For more information, call (415) 949-4888 or FAX (415) 949-1610.**

BUSINESS REPLY MAIL
FIRST CLASS   PERMIT NO. 884   LOS ALTOS, CA

POSTAGE WILL BE PAID BY ADDRESSEE

Crisp Publications, Inc.
95 First Street
Los Altos, CA 94022

NO POSTAGE
NECESSARY
IF MAILED
IN THE
UNITED STATES